সহিংখার গল্প

THE NUMBER STORY

SMALL BOOK ONE

ENGLISH - SYLHETI

Numbers Teach Children Their Number Names

written and illustrated by

MISS ANNA

Early Reader Edition of *The Number Story 1*
Bronze Medal Winner, 2016 Wishing Shelf Book Award

Library of Congress Control Number: 2018902040

Names: Miss Anna, author.
Title: Number story : numbers teach children their number names / Miss Anna.
Description: Portland, OR: Lumpy Publishing, 2018.
Identifiers: ISBN 978-0-9962164-7-0 | LCCN 2018902040
Summary: The pictures and rhymes present stories which introduce numbers 0-10.
Subjects: LCSH Numeration—English--Sylheti--Pictorial works--Juvenile literature. | BISAC JUVENILE NONFICTION /
Languages: English--Sylheti
Classification: LCC QA141.3 .M57 2018 | DDC 513—dc23

Publisher: Lumpy Publishing
Website: www.missannabooks.com
Email: missanna@missannabooks.com
Facebook: Miss Anna Lumpy

Paperback: ISBN 978-0-9962164-7-0
Printed in the U.S.A.   1 3 5 7 9 10 8 6 4 2

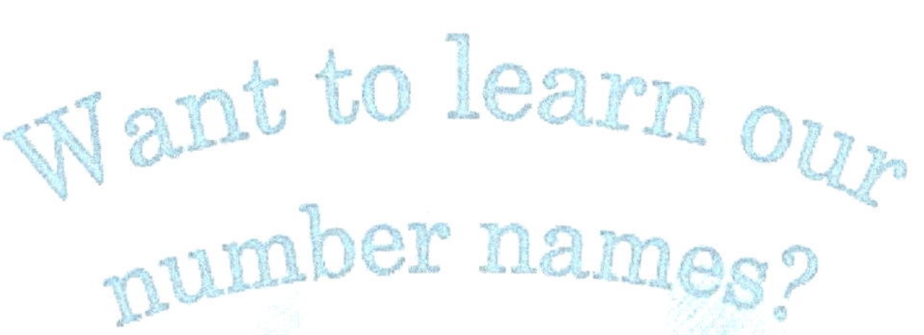

সইংখার নাম হিকতা চাইরা নি?

It is very easy and a lot of fun!

ইটা বেশী সুজা আর বহুত মজার!

Say-along our little jingle

চলোতে এক লগে গাই আমরার ছুট গল্প গুলা!

starting from Number One!

তে আমরা এক থাকি শুরু করি!

1

ONE   looks like my one finger.

১ ✩ এক

এক দেখতে আঙুলত্তর লাখান।

ONE!
এক!

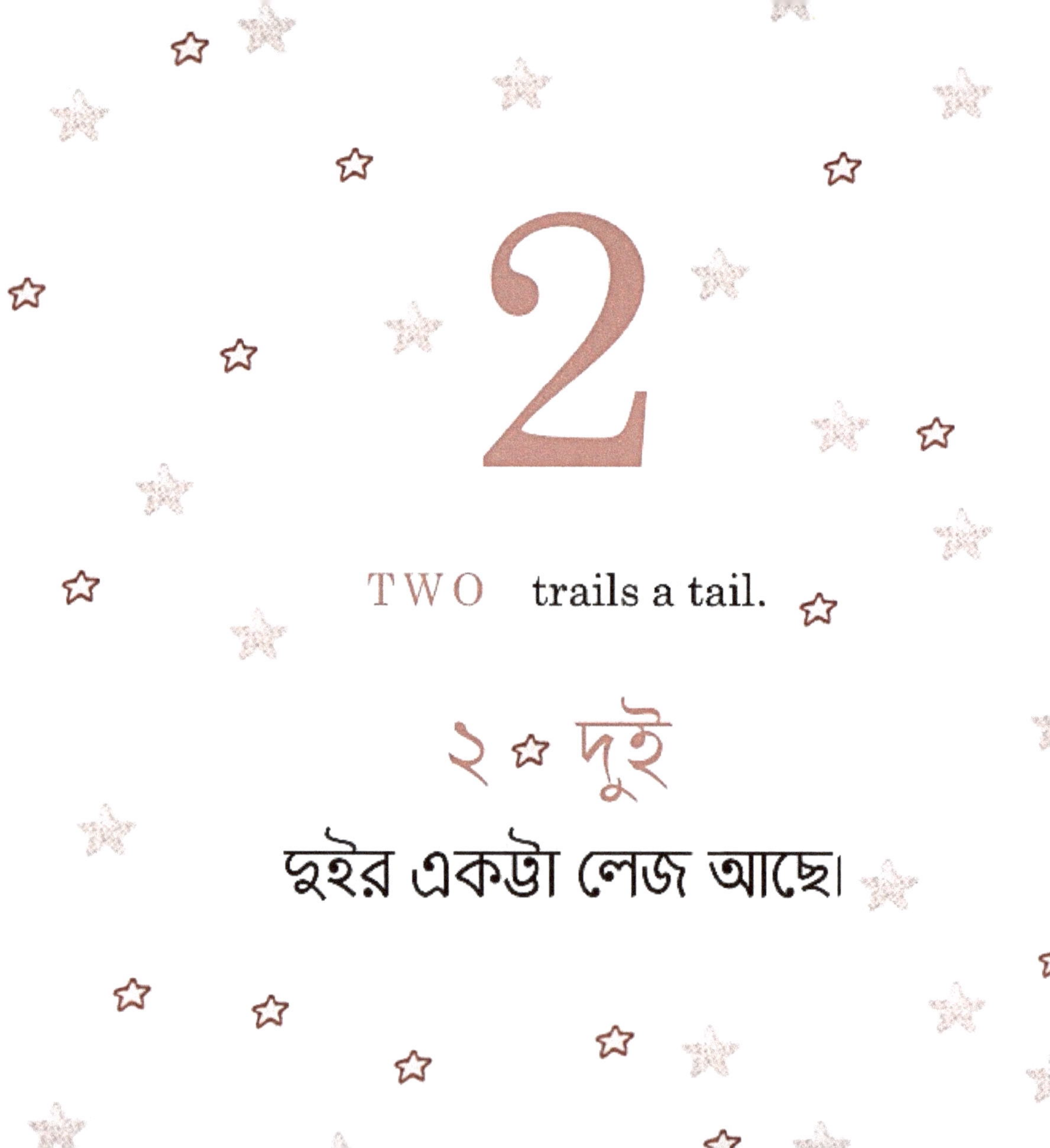
2

TWO   trails a tail.

২ ☆ দুই

দুইর একটা লেজ আছে।

A TAIL! একটা লেজে!

3

THREE has bumps.

৩ ☆ তিন

তিনঅর একটা কুঁজ আছে।

কুঁজর দিকে চাও!

4

FOUR   carries a sail.

৪ ☆ চাইর

চার একটা ডিঙ্গি নৌকা।

পাল উঠানি
নৌকার লাখান!

5

FIVE is a racing track.

৫ ✩ পাঁচ

পাঁচ একটা রেইচট্র‍্যর রোড।

VROOM
VROOM!
1

6

SIX   curves like a snail.

৬ ☆ ছয়

ছয় দ্যাখতে শামুকর মত।

A SNAIL! শামুক!

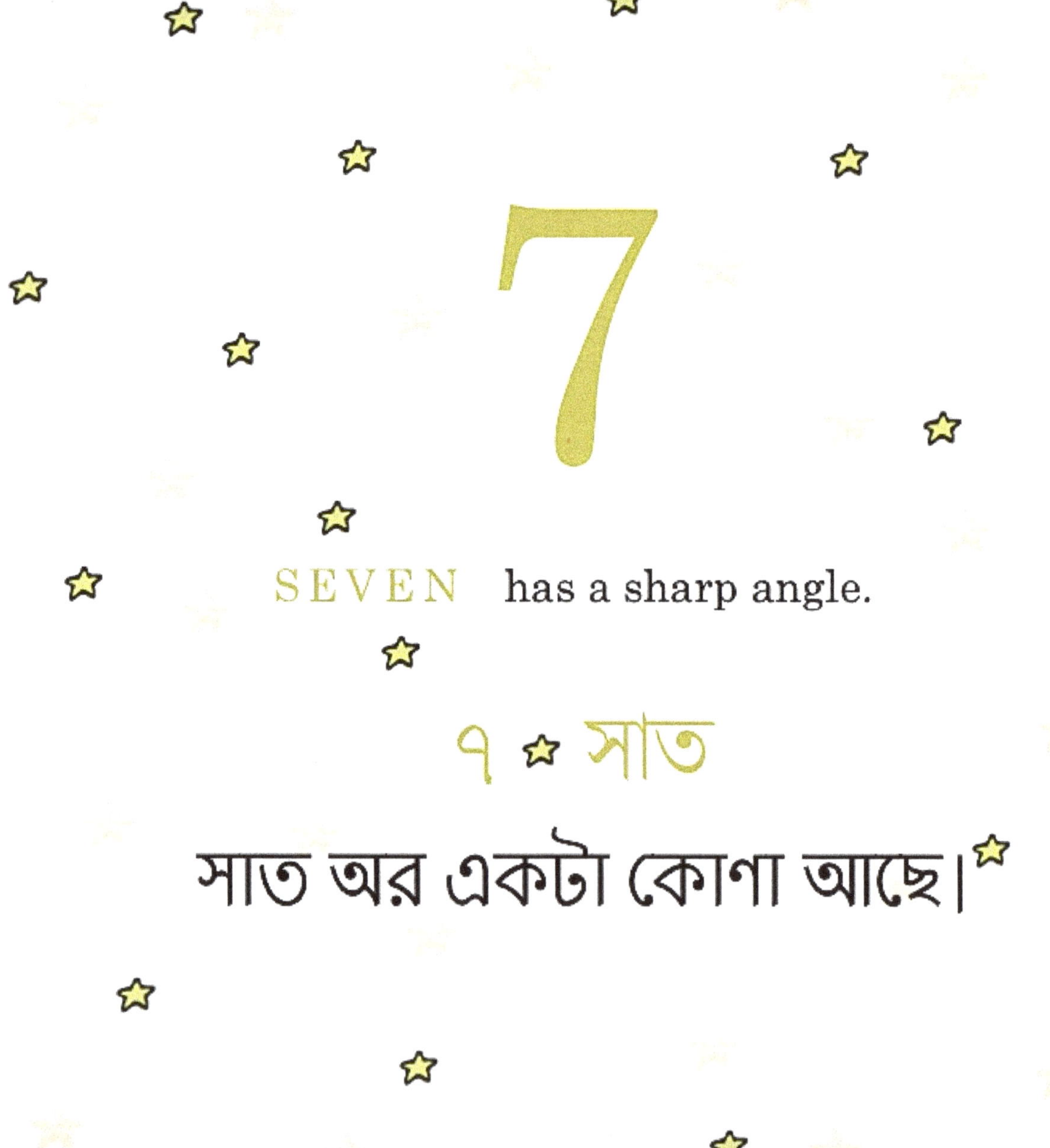

7

IT'S SHARP!

ইটা বহুত ধারাইল!

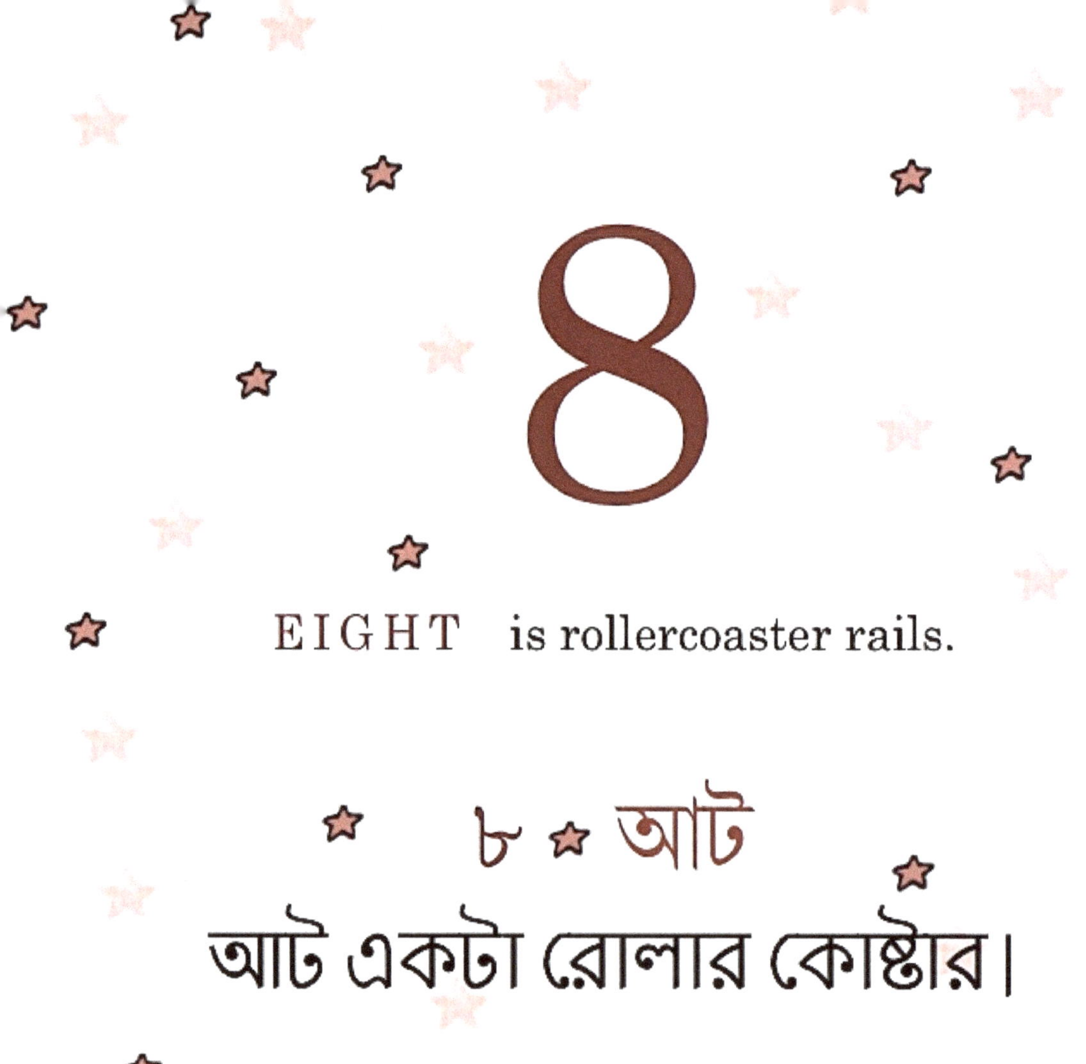

8
EIGHT   is rollercoaster rails.
৮ আট
আট একটা রোলার কোস্টার।

হুর্যাহ!
হুর্যাক্ষি!
YIPPEE!

9

NINE   is a bubble on a stick.

৯ ☆ নয়

নয় অইলে লাটির মাতাত
ফেনার লাখান।

A BUBBLE! বুদ্বুদ!

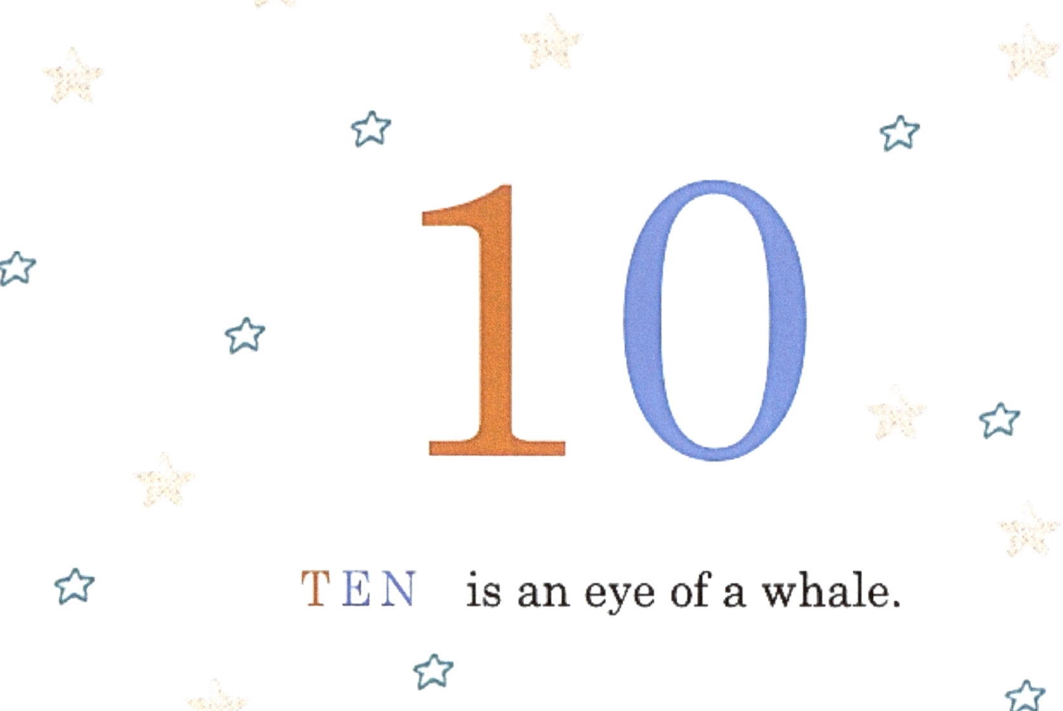

10

TEN   is an eye of a whale.

১০ ☆ দশ

দশ দ্যাখতে এক চূখা তিমির লাখান

HELLO! হ্যালো!

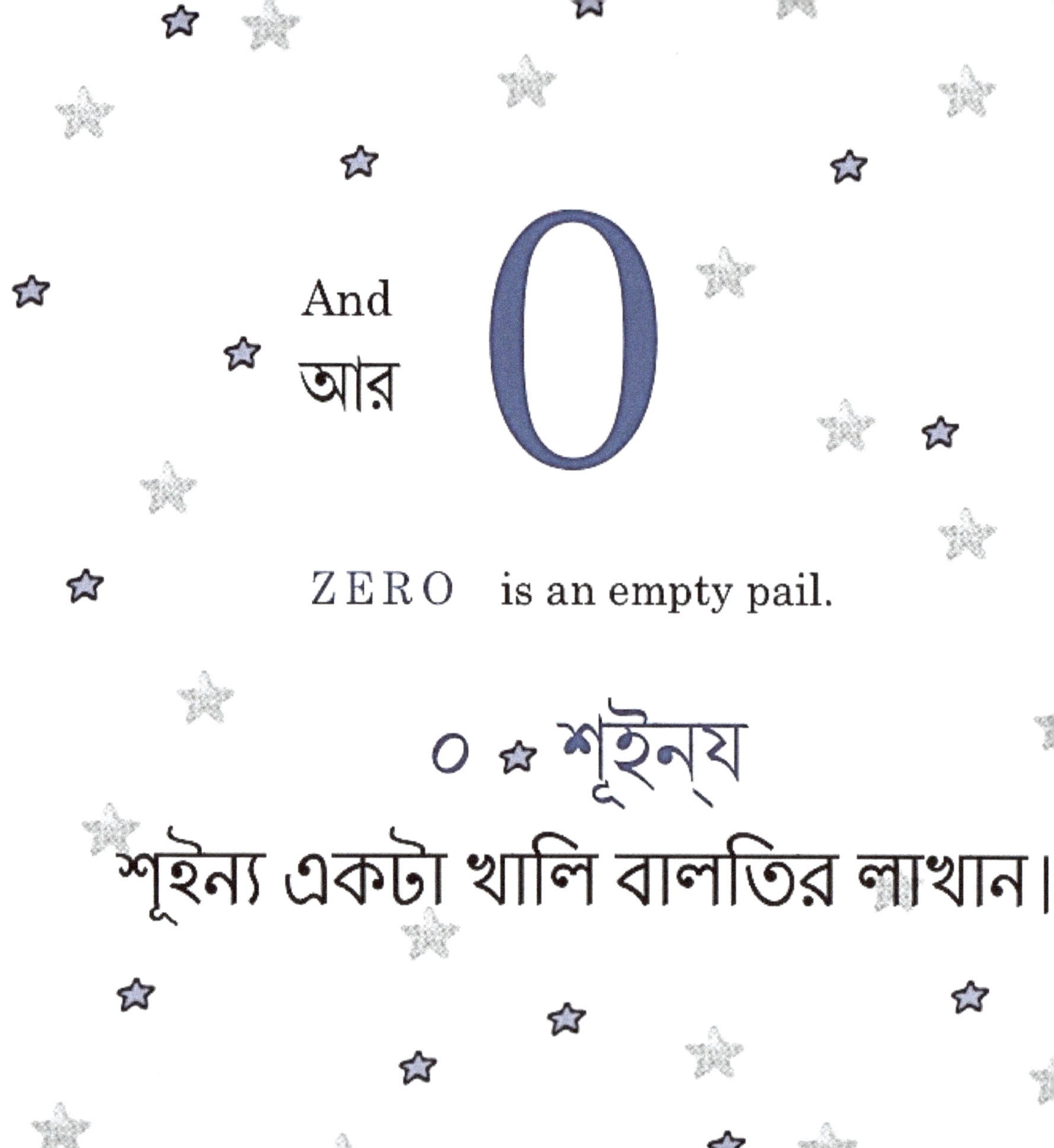
And
আর
0
ZERO   is an empty pail.
0 শূইন্য
শূইন্য একটা খালি বালতির ল্যাখান।

IT'S EMPTY!
ইটা খালি!

Thank you for playing with us today.

We had a lot of fun too!

ধইন্যবাদ, আমরার লগে আইজ খেলার লাগি।
আমরাও বহুত মজা পাইছি!

We are your Number friends,
Zero to Ten,
Who will be here for you~

আমরা তুমার সইংখা বন্ধু
শূন্য থাকি দশ।
আমরা সবসময় তুমার লগেও থাকি।

Bye-bye now!
See you again soon.

অখনের লাগি বাই!
আবার দেখা অইব নে!

The Numbers are *SINGING* too!

To sing-a-long, look for Miss Anna Number Story
at your favorite music store like iTUNES.

MP3

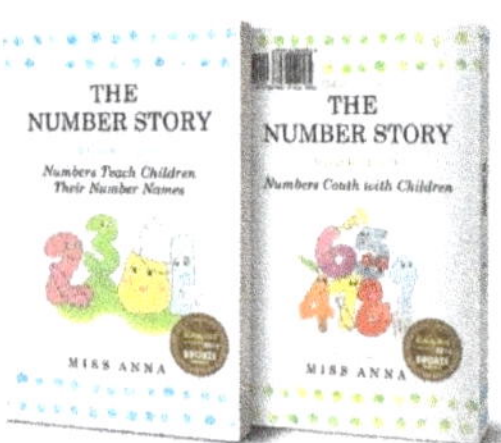

Numbers 0-10
IDENTIFYING
& COUNTING

Number Story 1 & 2

isbn: 978-0-996216-48-7

Numbers 11-20
& Ordinals

first, second, third...

Number Story 3 & 4

isbn: 978-1-945977-01-5

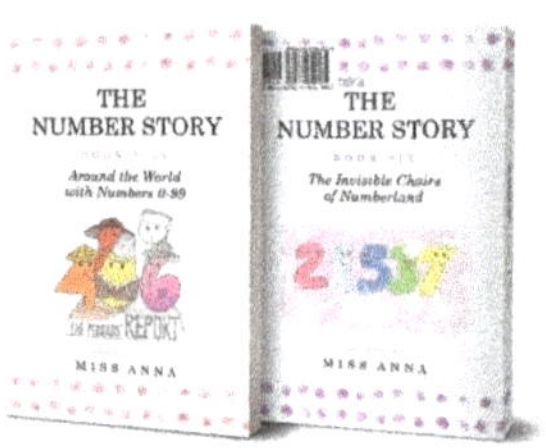

Numbers 0-100
& Place Values

ones, tens, hundreds...

Number Story 5 & 6

isbn: 978-1-945977-06-0

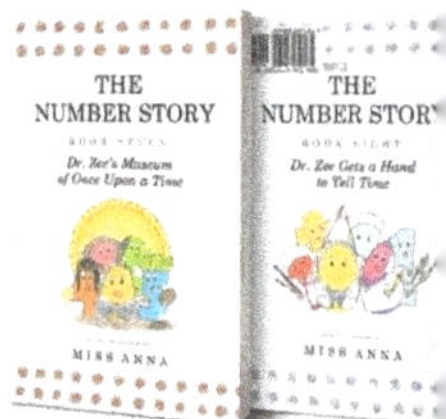

About Clock
& Telling Tim

hours, minutes, secon

Number Story 7 &

isbn: 978-1-949320-40

For more Miss Anna books to love,
visit us at

www.missannabooks.com

Numbers are working hard all over the world!
Come Travel the World with Us!